COLONIAL
FOOD

Verna Fisher

COLONIAL
QUEST

Nomad Press
A division of Nomad Communications
10 9 8 7 6 5 4 3 2 1
Copyright © 2010 by Nomad Press

This book was manufactured by
Regal Printing Limited in China
June 2010, Job #1005018
ISBN: 978-1-934670-99-6

Illustrations by Andrew Christensen

Questions regarding the ordering of this book should be addressed to
Independent Publishers Group
814 N. Franklin St.
Chicago, IL 60610
www.ipgbook.com

Nomad Press
2456 Christian St.
White River Junction, VT 05001
www.nomadpress.net

Contents

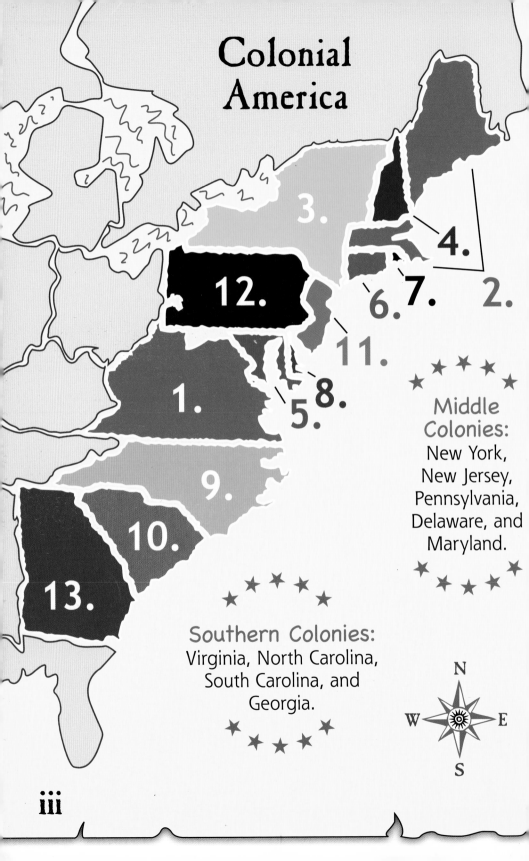

Colonial America

3.

12.

4.

6. 7.

2.

11.

1.

8.

5.

9.

10.

13.

Middle Colonies:
New York,
New Jersey,
Pennsylvania,
Delaware, and
Maryland.

Southern Colonies:
Virginia, North Carolina,
South Carolina, and
Georgia.

N
W ⊕ E
S

iii

New England:
Massachusetts,
New Hampshire, Connecticut,
and Rhode Island.

In the 1600s, people began leaving Europe to settle in America. Some were explorers searching for gold, while others came looking for freedom.

Jamestown in Virginia and Plymouth in Massachusetts were two of the earliest settlements where these people came to start a new life.

1. Virginia

2. Massachusetts

3. New York

4. New Hampshire

5. Maryland

6. Connecticut

7. Rhode Island

8. Delaware

9. North Carolina

10. South Carolina

11. New Jersey

12. Pennsylvania

13. Georgia

Surviving the Early Years

Can you imagine coming to a completely strange place with no grocery stores or restaurants?

Words to Know

colonist: a person who came to settle America.

New World: what is now America. It was called the New World by people from Europe because it was new to them.

What if you had to find or grow all of your own food? Sounds hard, right? That's just what the **colonists** had to do when they came to the **New World**.

The colonists found that many of the **crops** they grew in Europe did not grow well in **Colonial America**. The **climate** and growing seasons were different in the **colonies**.

Fruits that grew wild in America, such as cranberries and blueberries, were new to the settlers. At first, they weren't sure which were safe to eat.

During the early years, the colonists even struggled to catch fish. It was a difficult time. When winter came along, there was even less food. Many colonists did not survive their first winter in the New World.

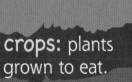

crops: plants grown to eat.

Colonial America: the name given to America when talking about the years 1607–1776.

climate: weather patterns in an area over a long period of time.

colonies: early settlements in America.

Words to Know

4

New Foods and Farming Techniques

The **Pilgrims** were a group of colonists who came to Massachusetts starting in 1620.

Pilgrims: people who came from England in the 1620s to settle Massachusetts.

Words to Know

In England,
Pilgrims had
been punished
for their beliefs.

The first Pilgrims arrived on a ship late in the year. They had very little time to prepare for the winter. More than half of the Pilgrims died from the cold and lack of food.

Luckily, the Pilgrims had help from a Native American man named Tisquantum. The settlers called him Squanto. He came from the Wampanoag tribe.

It took a lot of hard work to grow corn, harvest it, and grind the corn into cornmeal. After the colonists learned how to cook with corn from the Native Americans, they enjoyed cornmeal pancakes called johnnycakes.

Wampanoag: the Native American tribe of Tisquantum. The Wampanoag lived in the area where the Massachusetts colony was founded.

Words to Know

In the spring, Squanto taught the Pilgrims how to raise corn. Corn was a crop that did not grow in England. The colonists had been trying to grow English wheat, but had failed. The soil in Massachusetts was not good for growing wheat.

Squanto saved the lives
of the Pilgrims. In 1621, the
Pilgrims celebrated their good
harvest with a feast. Our
Thanksgiving is based on the
this first harvest feast!

The Pilgrims' harvest feast
lasted for three days. The Pilgrims
cooked many turkey and geese, while the
Wampanoag brought five deer. The meal
also included fish, clams, corn, carrots,
and onions.

The Native Americans did more
than just teach the colonists how
to grow corn and cook with it.
They also showed the colonists
new hunting techniques and
good places to hunt.

Before the meal, both the Pilgrims and
the Wampanoag gave thanks, each group
in their own way. Afterward, there was
plenty of good food, conversation, music,
and games to enjoy.

Different Regions,

What the colonists ate depended on where
they lived. Colonists who lived along the
coast ate lots of fish, crab, and clams.

Different Foods

Meanwhile, colonists in North and South Carolina consumed lots of sweet potatoes. Sweet potatoes grew well in these areas. They made sweet potato puddings and pancakes, and mashed sweet potatoes with butter.

Did You Know?

At first, sugar came from England. Later, the colonists got sugar from the West Indies, where slaves grew it on large farms called plantations.

Sugar came in solid, cone-shaped loaves. Colonists had to cut off a lump and grind it up before they could even measure it!

Then and Now

In colonial times sugar was an expensive luxury. It came by ship over long distances.

Today, sugar is a common ingredient that we use all the time and can buy at the store.

In New England, apples grew well. Colonists brought apple seeds with them from England in the mid-1600s.

Apples are good to eat straight from the tree. The settlers also turned ripe apples into delicious applesauce and apple butter.

Apple butter is applesauce that has been boiled down for a very long time, so it becomes thicker and develops a stronger flavor. Apple butter stays fresh longer than applesauce.

Words to Know

plantation: a large farm in a hot climate. In colonial times plantations had slaves for workers.

luxury: something that is not a necessity.

The colonists kept **livestock**, including cows and pigs. These animals gave the settlers milk, butter, and meat.

Gristmills were used to grind corn, wheat, and oats into cornmeal and flour. Mills were built next to a stream. The flowing water of the stream turned a large wooden wheel, connected to a grinding stone inside the gristmill. As the wheel turned, it transferred power from the water to the grinding stone. The grinding stone mashed the corn, wheat, or oats.

Words to Know

livestock: animals kept by people to give them food or to do work.

At the Table

In the early days of Colonial America, the settlers didn't have time to make furniture. They were too busy just trying to survive!

Colonists ate with knives or
spoons and even their hands.
The knives had pointed tips
for spearing pieces of food.

Dinner tables were very simple. The
colonists might even put wooden planks on
top of two barrels. People sat on stools or
benches.

Children ate their meal standing, while
the men sat in the few chairs.

Then and Now

In colonial times people put their cloth napkins over their shoulders.

Today, napkins are made of cloth or paper, and we put our napkins in our laps.

For plates, people used trenchers. These were squares of wood with hollows carved in their centers.

In some parts of America, trenchers and wooden plates and cups were used until the 1850s! Wealthier families also used plates and cups made out of clay or pewter.

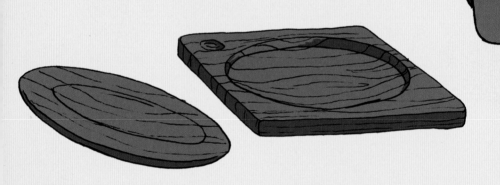

Words to Know

trencher: a piece of wood hollowed out and used instead of a plate.

pewter: a type of metal that is mostly tin.

Did You Know?

Have you ever heard someone call a kitchen "the heart of a home?" Is the kitchen a busy place in your house?

In colonial times, the kitchen was even busier. The kitchen fire was where women cooked meals and made candles, boiled water for baths and laundry, and warmed damp laundry. Something was always going on there!

Food of the Native Americans

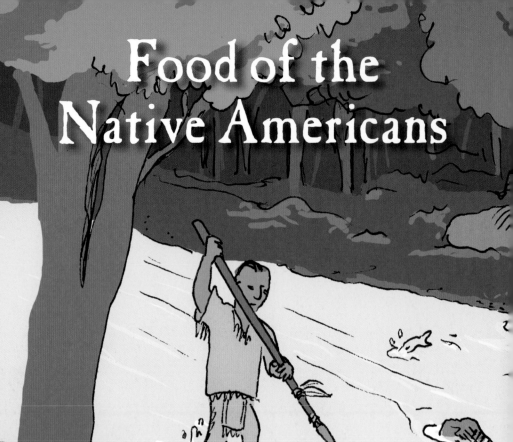

Native Americans were skilled at living off of the land. The Iroquois tribe often lived near rivers. They used spears or nets with handles to catch fish like salmon, herring, or trout.

Words to Know

smoking: drying meats and fish by hanging them in wood smoke.

preserve: to store food in a way that protects it from rotting.

By stringing large nets across a river, the Iroquois could collect a lot of fish at one time. The Wampanoag and Narragansett tribes lived near the ocean and ate clams, lobsters, and crabs.

At times of the year when fish were plentiful, many other tribes traveled to the ocean or rivers to catch fish. They smoked or dried these fish to preserve them. Then they brought the fish back to their villages to eat later.

Native American men were skilled hunters and trappers. They used spears or bows and arrows to hunt elk, moose, deer, ducks, geese, and turkey. The men also trapped beavers, foxes, rabbits, raccoons, and squirrels.

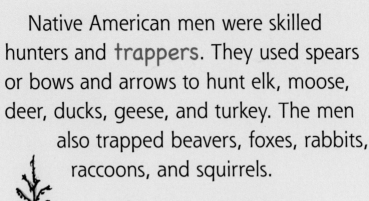

The Native Americans planted many crops. Corn was a major food source for the Native Americans.

The Iroquois planted corn, beans, and squash together. They called these plants the Three Sisters, because they get along well when they are planted together.

Spear and arrow points were made from stone, shell, or bone.

How do the Three Sisters get along? As the beans grow, they climb up the tall corn stalks. Meanwhile, the squash grows below the corn and beans. Its huge leaves shade the ground and prevent the soil from drying out and weeds from growing. Corn and beans together is a dish called succotash.

The Native Americans were grateful for the food they received from nature. They held festivals of thanksgiving many times a year.

trapper: someone who traps animals.

Words to Know

Glossary

climate: weather patterns in an area over a long period of time.

Colonial America: the name given to America when talking about the years 1607–1776.

colonies: early settlements in America.

colonist: a person who came to settle America.

crops: plants grown to eat.

livestock: animals kept by people to give them food or to do work.

luxury: something that is not a necessity.

New World: what is now America. It was called the New World by people from Europe because it was new to them.

pewter: a type of metal that is mostly tin.

Pilgrims: people who came from England in the 1620s to settle Massachusetts.

plantation: a large farm in a hot climate. In colonial times plantations had slaves for workers.

preserve: to store food in a way that protects it from rotting.

smoking: drying meats and fish by hanging them in wood smoke.

trapper: someone who traps animals.

trencher: a piece of wood hollowed out and used instead of a plate.

Wampanoag: the Native American tribe of Tisquantum. The Wampanoag lived in the area where the Massachusetts colony was founded.

Further Investigations

Books

Bordessa, Kris. *Great Colonial America Projects You Can Build Yourself.* White River Junction, VT: Nomad Press, 2006.

Fisher, Verna. *Explore Colonial America! 25 Great Projects, Activities, Experiments.* White River Junction, VT: Nomad Press, 2009.

Museums and Websites

Colonial Williamsburg
www.history.org
Williamsburg, Virginia

National Museum of the American Indian
www.nmai.si.edu
Washington, D.C. and New York, New York

Plimoth Plantation
www.plimoth.org
Plymouth, Massachusetts

America's Library
www.americaslibrary.gov

Jamestown Settlement
www.historyisfun.org

Native American History
www.bigorrin.org

Native Languages of the Americas
www.native-languages.org

Social Studies for Kids
www.socialstudiesforkids.com

The Mayflower
www.mayflowerhistory.com

Virtual Jamestown
www.virtualjamestown.org

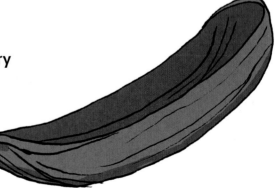

Index